# POPLAR

A Story

by

Are Simeon Thoresen

# POPLAR

A Story

*Written*
*In awareness*
*of trees*

by

Are Simeon Thoresen

*To All Who Search*
*To Understand*

**Translated from the Norwegian edition by Susanne Maria Dörfler**

ISBN-13: 9781519429544

ISBN-10: 1519429541

The book has been designed at CreateSpace ISBN.

Published by Amazon

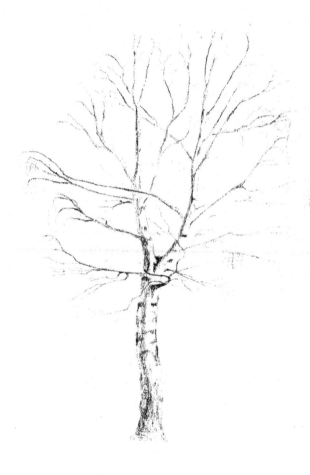

# Table of contents

7

# Part One

## How I met Poplar for the first time

Slowly my consciousness began to work again.

A ray of light, an orange shine dying.

A hint of fragrance vibrating in farewell

I tried to wake.

Memories began slowly to ache and rose like

nausea to the brain

All those who crossed my path

And visited my heart

Were wanderers like myself,

Fulfilling our karmic requirements.

The day fell and the stars were spread like the clouds.

All paths that were sleeping began to listen

for a new eternity.

Dust blew away from the footprints

Breakfast was easy to prepare: Bread, eggs and a glass of tea.

So there I was, a so-called natural therapist in a small town far up north, on the outskirts of an endless sea.
I had just turned 30 years old, having made a living as a natural therapist and veterinarian for some years.
Patients streamed in, but the actual *results* would not come. The results I had imagined. --- All those happy, joyous, thankful and newly-healed people and animals.

It bothered me that the percentage of healing was no more than about 40-50%, exactly what one could expect of the placebo effect. As if what I did had no effect at all!
I was worried, but smart enough to keep my worries to myself.
I actually could see positive effects on every other patient, and this gave me a better reputation than I expected. The rumor of something that happens is much more effective than if nothing happens at all.

I went outside into the garden.

It was a spring morning. The light green color reflected in the windows of the house. For a moment I wondered why I looked at the green color via its reflections in the windows and not directly out. Was this a fear of direct contact with life itself?

A cool wind blew up from the ocean, from the cold and watery inhospitable element. Up here in the north, many patients had problems with their kidneys, the reflection of the «water–element», so the inhospitality was both, inside and outside.

The mountains called "Børvasstindene" shaped a sharp horizon. The low birch trees tried to rise up again after the force of the hard winter winds and the heavy icicles.

The winter that never stopped coming back.

After I stood there and contemplated on this, it struck me that Kierkegaard had once said something like this:

Repetition is evolution....

Some redcurrant bushes and some low, crooked beech trees, something in between downy birch and dwarf birch, grew in this small and windy garden. The climate did not take good care of such plants in the north.

Then there was a poplar tree.

It was low, flimsy and windswept.

I had specified this tree and found out that it must belong to the family *Salicaceae* (willow–family). This family is called Salicaceae because some of its members contain salicylic acid, and is antipyretic. One of the tribes in these family is Populus (aspen) and a species group of this is the poplar-family.

I painstakingly tried to identify the species more exact. The poplar had single-sexed monoecious flowers in long hanging catkins, and small light seeds which spread in the wind with the help of soft white hairs. There are 35 species to choose from. Our most usual tree, *Populus tremula,* Eurasian aspen belongs to the poplar family. There is no other natural growing poplar in Norway. A few other species were planted in gardens and parks, for example the Silver Poplar (*Populus italica*), Black poplar (*Populus canadensis*), Virginia-poplar (*Populus virginiana*) and some types of Balsam poplars. By counting the number of stamen and other specific characteristics, I came to the result that the individual in front of me must be the northernmost growing male Silver Poplar one could find. Probably once planted by a homesick Italian.

After this, I took extra good care of this poor wretched freezing individual of a tree.

I longed for home myself, to a friendlier place more south.

#

Summer passed and autumn came.

I had moved south, to another small town at the outskirts of the sea, but this ocean was not endless and the surroundings were friendlier.

With me, in my moving load was the Silver Poplar.

My medical practice was still the same. Only that my percentage of healing rose from 40% to way over 60%.
I contemplated on this. I had learnt more, had more practice. Was this the reason for the increase?
However, I still did the same things. I stuck the same needles in the same acupuncture points and I prescribed the same homeopathic medicines and herbs.

One day I went out in the garden and looked at the little tree I had saved from the northern borderless regions, where the wind takes the ocean in, over the roofs.

I stood there for a while. The little tree that once was bent from the eternal winds blowing in from the sea, had begun to rise up. It had begun to grow larger and stronger and its silver color, which before was as cold as silver itself, had now gained a warm shimmer, like the downside of a raspberry-leaf.

With a sudden idea, I broke off a branch and took it inside. I put the branch in a pot with a piece of coal, poured half a liter of water over it and let it boil. After half an hour all water was boiled down, and the solids remained charred at the bottom of the pot. I did not really know what to do with this, but I scratched up the remnants into my hand.

It struck me that I could make a homeopathic medicine with this substance.

I brought the things I needed to my office. There was not very much. Some alcohol, some bottles and a book covered with leather. There is nothing to stop one from making one's own homeopathic remedies. It is actually a benefit if you can produce the substances by yourself, designed especially for the needs of the patient. The effects are much stronger if you make them yourself, something also Hahnemann, the founder of homeopathy had observed. I have often taught farmers about how to produce what they need and which substances they should use (willow–branches and charred birch wood) against diarrhea in calves.

This was what I intended to use this new remedy for: Chronic diarrhea.

If a plant is the basic substance, use 10 grams of plant material and put it into 100 grams of 30% alcohol, and let it steep for about a week. Sift the mixture and keep 10 grams of the liquid. Mix these 10 grams with 90 grams of water (1:9 ratio substance: water). Put this mixture into a bottle so that the liquid fills 1/2 –3/4 of it. Shake the mixture thoroughly for 2,5 to 3 minutes. It is helpful, to hit the bottle against some padded surface, (Hahnemann used his leather bible). I myself have tried this method, and a book bound in leather is perfect for this. By shaking vigorously the energy of the plant, the metal or other substances one wants to use as a homeopathic remedy, impregnates into the water. After shaking it, the bottle has to stand still for some minutes. You have now produced the potency D1 of the respective medicine. If you want to use it as D1, you have to conserve it because a watery drug will go bad quite quickly. Pour some alcohol into the mixture until it has 30% Vol. If you want to go on to get a D2, it will not be necessary to conserve it right now. Instead, you pour out nine parts of the D1 remedy and substitute them with water. Then you repeat the shaking procedure, and after the mixture has stood still for some minutes, D2 is ready. If you want to use it as a D2, conserve it as described above. This way you can work yourself up to D3, D4 and so on.

At last I had the substance as a D12 potency. What should I call it?

--Silur—

That was the name.

During the following days, I had strong feelings of the Silurian age.

15

I read about it from different sources.

One night I dreamt about it: I saw the old clouds soaring across the sky, the sun sending its light down to the earth and the stars talking their ancient silent language. I saw it from above, 80 million years ago. However, I woke from this special feeling, and these old times disappeared. The old times when the earth conceived the sunlight with innocence. When the earth was still an altar, not a grave. When humanity itself was only a star glimmering thought. It was difficult to come back to our time after this emotion, this dream....

Many years later, when I was sitting on the edge of a swimming pool far out in the countryside of Southern Florida, those feelings came over me again. I was there to teach American colleagues the art of pulse diagnosis. I stayed in the house of the organizer of the seminar and enjoyed her hospitality in the afternoons and evenings. The days lesson had ended, I was at peace. A tiny chameleon crept up on the round glass table in front of me, between the can of diet-coke and the cup of green tea. It sat motionless, for a long time. Every now and then, it blew up its bright red throat bladder; let it proudly play in the warmth, just to let it sink back into its motionless throat. Otherwise there were no other movements. Then, slowly, it turned its head and with intensive eyes it stared at me. Unfathomably. With an expression, I had never

16

seen before. We sat for a while like this, both equally still. I could see immemorable ages in those eyes, a depth of time with unsuspected proportions. The heat vibrated over the brown scorched pastures. The horses stood with heads hanging low in the shadow of a large oak tree that had huge amounts of Florida moss hanging from its branches. A herd of cows lay in the shadow of another oak tree. A mockingbird imitated his flying fellow creatures, whilst the lizard and I met eye to eye in ancient times.

Again, I felt "Silurian".

– And the old clouds still drifted on in the sky –

My patients with chronic diarrhea were content.


#


A year went by.

On inspiration I developed a new medicine made from the poplar tree, the Silver Poplar.

I had taken a square centimeter of its branch, and boiled it in a cup of water for 10 minutes. This infusion, if drunk daily over a long time, will make an over dimensioned prostate decrease. I treated many elderly men with 'weak jets' during the years after this discovery, and most of them took a great pleasure in this tea.


#


I became constantly more and more aware that I had some kind of help with my therapy. It felt more and more like someone was whispering in my inner ear.

It could be like a notion, as if I already knew what would happen, or how I was to treat my patients.

It could be like something changing the direction of my hand, when I was about to set a needle into an acupuncture point. More and more often, I had chosen a point, but when I was putting the needle in, it felt, like something took over my consciousness, and the needle was put somewhere else.

One day I had decided to hand out a certain remedy to a patient, and was on my way to the closet to get this special medicine. Suddenly everything seemed to go black before my eyes. All the light seemed to concentrate on a completely different bottle than the one I had previously chosen. Almost like a somnambulist, I took this bottle and gave it to the patient.

It proved to be the right medicine.

# Part Two

## How Poplar withdrew

I was calm, and convinced I had evolved as a therapist.

However, there was something worrying me. Some things were out of my control, something beyond my understanding. It felt like I did not evolve because of my own efforts, but that "something" evolved me, or evolved inside of me.
This small voice inside my head, which often told me what I should do.

I increasingly felt that I had to find out about this.

I was out in the garden, wandering around silently, and felt nature surrounding me. The clouds drifted in the sky bringing up the old "Silurian" feeling, causing me to float away, but the birds held me back in the present moment. Their song kept me from totally leaving the present time, and the warmth of the summer made my emotions vibrate, made them alive.

Suddenly a little stone jumped right up in front of my feet, from the left to the right. I stopped and wondered.

Did I see right? It felt like I was shaken out of my usual consciousness; as if the light took on a different nuance, the sounds a different value, like the fragrances of a yet unknown dimension.

A low humming sound behind me made me turn my head. Slowly the rest of my body followed. The humming slowly emerged into a low song. It was the poplar tree singing.

-- the poplar tree sang --

I stood and listened.
The thought that I should actually be spellbound crossed my mind, but strangely I was not. Everything seemed so natural, so right and above all so unbelievably beautiful. I felt my eyes filling with tears and wanted to move with the music, to conduct.
Then I heard another voice. A duet arose, when the plum tree beside it also began to sing. I was awed. A stinging pain crawled up my leg, as if a snake had bit me under the foot.

Pain and joy.

Soon after, the whole garden sang in the choir. It felt as if the choir of Beethoven's 9th symphony surrounded me.

After an indeterminate time the song became quiet, and I sank into stillness.

-- then Poplar spoke —

I still do not know what he said, but it poured inside me like a silent stream.
I answered, or asked.
He explained, or spoke.
I do not know which, and I do not know for how long.

In the end, I stood there and all was over. It was evening. I must have been standing there for several hours.

I do not know any more.

However, I was clearly aware of what he had told me.
He informed me in countless ways that I "*must not pass him*", must not *"go past him"*.
I must not pass him. He expressed himself very clearly, that I must not pass him.

Even today, I do not fully comprehend the meaning of this[1].

---

[1] *A further revelation and extention of this knowledge of Poplar is described in the book "Atlantis", (The Forgotten Mysteries of Atlantis In times of the destruction, Refound in present day Ireland through Anthroposophy, and their Karmic importance for today), published by Are Thoresen on Amazon 2015.*

I have contemplated and thought about this many times, and I have understood the meaning of his teachings, his knowledge in several ways.

It took a long time before I could even guess what he meant, because I never had an explanation.
He never spoke to me again in such a direct way as he did that summer day in the garden. It was a one-time experience. But the message was clear.
Unfortunately, I did not understand it until a long time after.
Not until I had made many mistakes, which lead me in countless wrong directions.

Two months later, I got the first hint about what Poplar had meant.
I was visiting a colleague who worked in a small town further south. He told me that he wanted to expand his office and employ more people. By doing this he could work less, have more time off, experience less stress.

Suddenly Poplar appeared in front of my spiritual eyes.

He appeared as a representative for nature's inner life. As an icon for all that lives of its own accord, all created by itself, by its own meaning.

Suddenly I became aware of one aspect of Poplar's wisdom. That I should not go over the boundaries life creates.

I did not understand more at this point.

I continued with my life and my practice as before.

# Part Three

## How darkness broke out

I woke up again.

Slowly my consciousness began to work.

A ray of light, an orange shimmer of dying penetrated my mind.

A hint of fragrance vibrating in farewell with life ached in my soul.

Something was lost. I just did not know what it was.

A few weeks later, it was clear, too clear. So painfully clear.

The days at the office had become a pastime. I could no longer figure out what I was supposed to do. I no longer knew what I should be doing. I had become a recipe-book practitioner.

The scientific fact was that the percentage of healing I achieved was down to 40% again.

Inspiration had vanished.

The voice, the inner leading guidance was lost.
Painfully I realized why and where this voice had come from.

It had come from Poplar.

It had been a connection to the tree, maybe to trees in general, to the whole of nature, which had led me.
Now, when I met Poplar, his voice was silent. It felt like the song-meeting had made our contact invisible.
Like lovers, who do not have anything to say to each other after their first passionate night.

No, I did not like that comparison.

My thoughts wandered to the Norwegian fairytales.

There was always a boy, who met the princess. Their first encounter was often a coincidence, without him deserving it, without him doing anything to achieve it, without him being actually interested.
There was always a room he should not enter, or something he was forbidden to do.
If he entered the room, the princess would disappear.
It was as if, when a person came into contact with something spiritual or magic, the magic disappeared.

After talking with Poplar and receiving insights about the life of the plant-world, my contact with them disappeared.

I began to contemplate more about fairytales.

After the princess had disappeared, the poor boy had to find her again. To be able to do this he had to work really hard. He had to remember what she had said and this time he had to follow her advice.

Was it by remembering and following what he had said I could re-find him? Could I reestablish my contact with poplar?
What was it Poplar had said? That I should not pass him?
I had to try to understand the full meaning of his wisdom. Maybe I could then find him again, find the princess again.

What could it mean "to go past him"?

Go past nature?
Do not show consideration towards trees?
Go past my own abilities? My natural abilities?

The following days, weeks and months I strived to understand. To understand what Poplar had meant.

Three years passed.

The process of first loosing the contact to nature and then trying to reconnect was decent to hell. In the end, I became sick, got pneumonia and was totally exhausted.

The decent started with depression, I felt lonely and deserted.

All my friendships seemed to be without meaning. I felt they were outside of me, as if I could never contact them again.
One evening in my loneliness, I looked up to the sky and observed the thousands of stars. It might be that people and friends were without meaning; they could come and go through time, only the stars were eternal, they were important, those I could trust.

This insight calmed me down for exactly three days.

In the evening of the third day, when I again directed my gaze to the stars in the sky, a horrible thought struck my mind. The light of those stars, those bodies in the cosmos, those faithful following friends, had been on their way to my eyes for years, maybe thousands of years. In this very moment, they might not exist anymore. They could be dead, for all I knew. Their light was only a mirage, an illusion, a memory impregnated into matter.

I never saw the "real" stars.

I felt more alone and deserted than ever before.

It was not until a few months later that I started to feel a certain security again. I still had myself, and my emotions. If all was insecure, if all else was gone; my emotions were mine.
This thought comforted me for some weeks, but then I became uncertain again. Emotions were unsteady, they were influenced by time and surroundings. The more I thought about it, the more it seemed that my emotions were strangers to me, and in the end, I felt as if they were only borrowed colored balloons. Blown up balls, hovering in front of me like those in an amusement park or circus.

Whatever the case, my emotions were not me.

In this situation, weakened by doubt and loneliness, unable to reestablish my contact with nature, with Poplar, I went to Florida to host a workshop in natural therapy.

It was September and the building I worked in had no air-conditioning.

After one week I was exhausted, completely spent by diarrhea and close to a heatstroke.
I barely remember anything of the return flight home.
I fainted several times, and felt that there was not much life left in my body.

However, there was a tiny white flame inside my heart.

I stumbled out into the garden and stood there for a while to regain full consciousness. I felt weak, inadequate and dying.

In this situation, my eye fell on Poplar.

He stood there so innocent and waiting.

I felt time slowly lose its meaning. Seconds became minutes without the experience of time following it. The distance between Poplar and myself became small and large at the same time and lost all its significance.
It was as if realization of time and assessment of distances melted together until I no longer could separate which was time and which was distance. The sphere became two-dimensional or maybe five-dimensional when eternity wove itself in and tightened depth and time.

A simmering warmth, a new awareness poured into my mind.

It was now clear to me what the deeper meaning of Poplars message meant. It was not that I *must not pass him*, but that *I should not believe that I had passed him.*
Trees have been on this Earth for immemorable times, much longer than we have. They have developed intelligent systems for nourishment, propagation and all

processes that life demands. They are able to live and breathe without the organs we depend on, the organs, which cause us so much pain, sickness and death. They grow without being burdened with fat depots, which make us humans ill. They survive the cold with intelligent mechanisms, while we die after just a few hours in winters freezing temperatures.

In short, trees are far superior to us humans.

Moreover, they have their own communication system. They sing songs together as do the biggest choirs we can imagine. They communicate with each other and try to teach us humans their secrets without us being aware of what they say.

The certainty that Poplar was a much more advanced entity than humans made me dizzy.

I crept into my bed, shivering.

# Part Four

## How I became healed

Slowly my consciousness began to work again.
A ray of light, an orange shimmer that slowly grew stronger.
A weak vibration was felt as I reunited with the living.

I had a dream.

I sat in a room, alone. It was evening. Someone entered. I was not afraid and I took a message from those miraculous beings that had entered. My world was at peace, and I experienced old memories in me, those old memories that break and bend in one's mind. However, I knew that this must be my path, if eternity would be mine. I rose in an uncertain calmness as they danced their dance. They whirled around in the holy circle but it looked more as if they were being pulled away. I sank down in the moonshine, I knew they had to leave before the dawn, before the rebirthing sun broke their peace.

It was hard to wake up.

# THE SUBTERAINIENS

It breathes softly in the hill and in the moss

The sun has gone down.

They come in, in a silver grey shine

My world is at peace

And know the old in me

Breaking and bending in the mind

But this must be my path

If eternity should be mine

I raise in uncertainty

They whirl around in their holy circle

I'm sinking down in the moonshine

I know they have to leave

Before the dawn with the sun in its mind

Breaks their peace

I remembered the previous day. I was in the garden. The doors to the house were closed, or was it the doors back to the civilization I once knew, that I once had believed in. There was a window in one of the doors. I balanced between being inside and outside. That was how I felt. Not far away was Poplar. Suddenly it was as if the tree smelled, as if it was filled with fragrance and flowers. As if the white full moon had sent her rays down on us. I felt newly washed, like on a Saturday. Close to the trunk of the tree stood a spirit in the moonshine, and even though it was daytime and all the others slept, the spirit shone in the dark.

I can't remember any more.

After this I recovered quickly.

The voice, the connection to nature was back. My relationship with Poplar had begun to work again, after I acknowledged his superiority.
Acknowledged, that he has been on this earth longer than me, much longer.
Acknowledged that he was as important and advanced as I was.

After this, my success rate in healing suddenly jumped up to 80%, and even 90% ...... and it was not because I had been to a new seminar or course ......

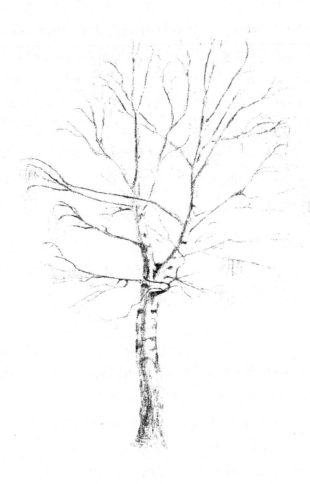

# Part Five

## The Element Of The Trees

In the year 1985, I went hiking in the mountains. There I suddenly saw snake-like streams of black, waving and streaming «power lines». They looked like black shiny snakes meandering around the rocks.

Later I could see them in the forest and also close to the ocean.

They were connected to the trees, not only to one tree but to all trees ....

Later, in the winter, whilst I was skiing in the deep Norwegian woods, this network appeared again in front of my eyes with all its grandness and complexity.

I will describe it as some kind of matrix weaving between the trees, actually weaving between all living entities, and that included nearly the whole world. Dark snakes like water-streams, all with different strengths and thicknesses. This matrix of black snakes was interwoven within all nature, including the farms I passed by, the trees, everything alive. I saw how these power lines streamed forth from the woods, embracing barns, cows, pigsties and houses. Wherever there were animals, the contact was stronger than where there were none. Maybe this is the reason we feel so connected to animals and nature. We feel ourselves as part of a greater correlation to the whole (which of course we are).

These power lines went from tree to tree and from human to tree. They were stronger between trees belonging to the same species, between animals of the same species, between men.

This experience made me aware that the entire creation is woven together in one grandiose, cosmic togetherness, and if something changes or disappears, it will affect us all. If one thing in this entirety suffers, the whole cosmic entirety will suffer.

When the sun shines on the trees, the center of the streaming energy, the tree-energy is about 2/3 from the ground, and focused towards the sun. In the night the center is 1/3 from the ground, and focused towards the earth, downwards. Therefore, as I am on the ground, I feel contact with this ethereal world much better at nighttime or in the shadows. The trees do not pay so much attention to the moon. At night they communicate more with each other and with me.

When I rode out into the woods one day, I almost became jealous of Balder, my horse. His communication with the trees was about ten times stronger than mine. It seems as if animals are much closer to the ether-streams of plants than we humans are. Many claim that horses can feel the plants they eat, they know which ones are poisonous and which are beneficial. If a plant has lost its ether–streams, is dead, the animal can no longer feel which is poisonous or not.

The trees try to communicate with people skiing as they do with me, only those on skis do not pay attention. They close off to the communication. It is sad to see that so many people are training/jogging in the forest today, yet so few walk and feel the trees.

As told earlier the main center for the energetic field of the trees (their center for communication) is about 1/3 up on their trunk during the night, 2/3 up during the day. Some trees have both centers active at the same time.

All my life I have felt a strong affiliation with trees; now I can understand why. It is the same with animals, but not as strong as with trees.

Some groups of trees seem to show a certain familiar group affiliation. Then the power of many trees is gathered together and concentrated within one single tree, their "leader", which is most often the tree that communicates with me.

There is another energy structure I have observed. This I discovered on February the 24th 2004. This structure is like a whirlwind circling around each individual being, like the clothes of a dervish–dancer. I almost had the feeling that if I could make this spiral structure go faster, it would work like a wing, a helicopter propeller, and I would be able to levitate.

Moreover, the trees that stand closer to bigger roads have a stronger contact or interest in the passing cars than those standing further back, who are not interested at all.

Generally, it is obvious that most of the trees are not very interested in human doings and strivings. At least not in those two energy–structures I have observed.

#

When I was younger I read about Indian tribes, who believed that the word's wellbeing and existence was dependent on their specific tribe, and that it was of utmost importance they continued to do their religious rituals.

When I woke up on the morning of March 20th 2004, a deep realization dawned on my mind. I had been wandering inside this holistic network of energetic streams since February 24th 2004, actually more or less since the summer of 1985, feeling increasingly as a participant in this network, as an inseparable part of this matrix. I had in the end an absolute awareness that I was an inseparable part of the entire cosmos.

If I disappeared, the total creation would not be the same.

Then I understood the meaning of the Red Indian's mindset.

And I understood that this "childish" attitude was a result of the great cosmic experience they had of all–nature, as a people of nature, having walked in this holism all their lives.

# An open door

A door

Can only be opened

Where there is a crack in reality,

like a keyhole

is a crack in the door blade.


A crack changes something.

Impossible things may happen,

like the laws of physics mingle

Or are reversed.

A crack is the door to another dimension.

All transcendental  perceptions

begins with finding this crack.

That we find the keyhole,

Turn the key -

Which is our own soul.

Trees that are planted in cities have much less ether-streams than those growing in woods. In addition people in cities scarcely have contact with these streams. Probably it is my feeling of community with the trees, which brings me so much joy when being out in nature. People who do not have this realization, or are not in contact with trees are unable to experience this joyous feeling when they wander through the forest.

#

The year 2006 had come, bringing warmth and spring. Resin rises up in the trees leading to the thick energetic streams splitting up into a delicate network of smaller streams, weaving themselves throughout the entire tree, especially visible in the outer sprouts. It resembles the appearance of a veil.

This was the third network I experienced.

One morning, when I went to Balder with some hay, his energy-lines began to form a circle around his head, like a circling wreath, like a maelstrom, but not as fast. It stayed like this until he had eaten. Then this activity moved further down towards the stomach.

When I went back into the house, my eye caught a crow sitting on the rooftop. It had an energy-structure, which was similar to the one Balder had around his head whilst eating.

It was like a horse head.


*June 2006;*

Through springtime, the new (third) net of energy I had observed focused more and more towards the sun and the coming summer. It looked like the matrix I observed during wintertime had disappeared. However, in the beginning of June I realized that this was not the case. The dark snakelike network merely had split into two parts; one part focusing on the sun and the life-giving light, and the other forming the already described network. It was as if the trees had both an etheric and an astral energy-network, which in winter melted together to create one single network. I could then not divide the ethereal and the astral. In spring and early summer the two energy structures separated and could be observed more specifically.


*July 2006;*

I went for a walk in the forest in rainy weather. I saw that the tree's upwards going energy-structure, which usually is focused on the sun, now was bent downwards like some sort of umbrella and almost looked like a mushroom. In the rain, when photosynthesis diminishes, the trees look rather like mushrooms, an entity that has no photosynthesis.

Throughout the whole summer it became clear that the trees had a network that went upwards and depended on the sun, and one that goes downwards relating to the earth. The latter is the one I observed during the winter.

The different trees also have different and individual networks, both dependent on species and individuality. The different individuals of a species communicate with each other with varying intensity. They also communicate with other species, but this is much less than within the same family.

The whole forest is a very dynamic and living phenomena of energetic patterns.

*March 2007*

Today, when the clock showed 06:25 I woke up and my observation of nature's networks was fundamentally enlarged. Until now the energy-network had been mostly black. Now it suddenly turned white. When I went out for a walk later that day, it was like walking through fireworks. The trees were covered with sparkling fireworks. I realized after a while that the black streams still were there, but now the white light streams outshone them.

I think the astral streams of the trees became part of my consciousness for some days in march 2007. This network is chaotic, shifts quickly and is glistening. Those days I felt the same.

When I went out into nature it felt like walking in a fountain of light, an ocean of light.


A strong and crazy feeling.



*March 2007*

The same differentiation I observed with the black energy network from 1985 (which became differentiated in 2006/7) now begins to happen to the white glistening ocean of light. It becomes more and more structured and I recognize forms and structures in a higher degree than during the first few days. It overwhelmes me and I wander around as if I am in a different world. Also now, I can see that the black network has not vanished but coexists with the white one, only the white one outshines it, as the sun outshines the moon.


I think this comparison is more real than just a comparison. However, the future will tell.

I want to add another interesting observation here:

Several times, I have watched anglers or hunters. They are usually unaware of their connectedness with nature. In a way, they are alone in nature. However, by taking a life, by killing a living being, suddenly their connection to creation opens up and for some minutes they are a part of the whole. This might be the reason why hunters so often justify their hunting activities by saying that it gives them a good "experience" of nature. When I went to veterinary school I often discussed this, particularly with my fellow students, why one has to kill to experience nature, instead of just being out in nature. Now I understand. Because they do not have the nature connection "naturally", they have to kill to experience it. The same way the role of the victim is explained in many ancient religions and mysteries. With the lamb's blood running out, a connection is made to the spiritual world and it feels like the Gods come closer.

Of course, it is better to have this nature connection all the time, without having to kill somebody ...

# Part Six

## Dimensions Are Woven In

Winter came again and the outer side of summer was replaced with our inner eye. The expansion of the trees in space and the communication of all individuals of the creation were led into the dimension of time.

It started quite simple. December 10th 2008 I sat at my mother's sickbed. She was 95 years old. Whatever she said was meaningless, and I did not pay much attention. Suddenly I felt a strong contact with her, a sort of embrace, our bodies became woven together and I drifted into a sleeplike condition.

Time began to roll in my inner eye and I saw things that happened before, but with her perspective .. I was one with her. I *was* her.

I saw that I was born, was small, grew, grew, ... grew. I came home for lunch after school, after college, after high school ...

After 10 minutes, I "woke up".

I never had experienced a closer contact with my mother. What had happened?

After a few days I began to understand what it could have been. Now that my mother was lying on her death bed, I no longer felt the need to "stand up" against her, be an individual being in front of her or be compelled to break free from a parent like her. I could let it all go.

She was so weak that our energies could freely weave into each other's. I experienced the memories which were in her soul, in her aura, in her etheric body.

Then ... a few days later I went out in the woods ....

I thought that maybe I could experience the same with the trees as I did with my mother. The words of an old song came into my mind;

*Pay the cost of freedom*

*Lay your body down*

*Mother earth will swallow you*

*Buried in the ground*

When I was 20 years old I had translated this text into Norwegian, as if I already knew what the future would bring, would be experienced...

*Betal hva frihet krever*

*Legg deg sakte ned*

*Kjenn naturen lever*

*Døden bringer fred*


I put on some warm clothes, went out to the forest in the evening and lent myself against a tree. I tried to eradicate myself as an individual, somehow like choosing the individual death.
After a while things started to move around me. Shapes took form... like mist ...

Again, time rolled backwards, backwards.

Clear imaginations of tree forms, ferns, lost ages, giant ferns, clear sky, a world without pollution... a word came to my mind....

....... Silur ......

I began to feel cold, rose – and went home.

The next day when I was more awake, it struck me, that it was maybe all just an illusion. An illusion that I needed a tree, that I needed to lean on a tree to get into their ethereal world. I only needed to *want* it, to *intend* to do it...

I tried to do this, to observe the thick black snakelike forms and somehow step into them. I quit observing them, but tried instead to feel them. I went from observation to communication. At once leaf forms appeared in my consciousness. Large finger-shaped leaves, high trunks, colors, mostly greens. All shapes moved and melted into each other. It felt like I was floating or swimming in an ocean of forms and nuances of green.
Simultaniously time conception was changed. Different varieties of animals and plants belonging to distant historical ages appeared. I was in a waving sea of ether without the limitation of time. It was like entering a "Lost World", but I was uncertain how this happened.

Is this the part of the world that is called the Akashic Chronicle?

How can I keep orientation in this world?
How can I follow tracks and paths?
How do I find tracks and paths?

The next day it came to my mind. Each individual has its own world, its own part of the lost world. If I enter, for example, the ethereal world of a horse, a human being, or a mineral instead of the trees maybe I could enter the Akashic Chronicle of those beings.

Completely different stories ....

During the next months, I experimented with different methods to enter the ethereal streams of other beings.

Again, a horseback ride in the forest gave me new insights. I rode "Donegal", I tried to enter the ethereal streams I saw between the horse, the trees and the plants. When I finally succeeded, I experienced all growth around us as expressions of taste in addition to the normal impressions like sight and sound. The special thing about those taste-impressions was that they occurred in the belly, at the diaphragm, and not in the mouth, as is the case with normal taste experiences.

I took a trip up to the top of the hill one winter evening, when the sun began to set. I lit a fire, and lay down beside it while some sausages slowly warmed up.
As I lay there and observed the ethereal streams between the trees that are always stronger in winter, I realized that what I had previously described as energetic streams, were actually tubes; hollow cylinders and not streams. Everything consists of tubes or tunnels, just like the tunnel we see immediately after death. A tunnel we have to go through to enter another dimension where we meet a strong light, or a bright shining person. It seems that there is always a tunnel that leads to

another dimension. Once I have entered these ethereal streams I then have to reach for the inner void where I enter a kind of tunnel. Then I am inside the ethereal world, inside a different dimension where I can freely move, independent of time through the Akashic Chronicle.

I start to wonder if one can be reborn regardless of time …

I would like to describe the "black ethereal streams" a little more. When I enter them and allow myself to become one with them, the following happens:
I first have to switch off my thoughts, allow myself to be guided and step out of time. I then exist outside of time. All is then simultaneously in present, past and future. I am filled with the feeling of oneness. I can clearly see that I am one with everything, but nevertheless I experience myself as an individual center.
This center is in both my heart and in my spiritual insight.
And I understand that to be able to go further inside this ethereal world I have to understand who I am, understand myself.

It strikes me, that this experience is the mirror image of the Mantra Rudolf Steiner[2] gave as one of his most fundamental insights:

---

[2] **Rudolf Joseph Lorenz Steiner** *(27 (25?) February 1861 – 30 March 1925) was an Austrian philosopher, author, social reformer, architect, and esotericist. Steiner gained initial recognition at the end of the nineteenth century as a literary critic and published philosophical works including The Philosophy of Freedom. At the beginning of the twentieth century, he founded an esoteric spiritual movement, anthroposophy, with roots in German idealist philosophy and theosophy; other influences include Goethean science and Rosicrucianism. In the first, more philosophically oriented phase of this movement, Steiner attempted to find a synthesis between science and spirituality; his philosophical work of these years, which he termed spiritual science, sought to apply the clarity of thinking characteristic of Western philosophy to spiritual questions, differentiating this approach from what he considered to be vaguer approaches to mysticism. In a second phase, beginning around 1907, he began working collaboratively in a variety of artistic media, including drama, the movement arts (developing a new artistic form, eurythmy) and architecture, culminating in the building of the Goetheanum, a cultural centre to house all the arts. In the third phase of his work, beginning after World War I, Steiner worked to establish various practical endeavors, including Waldorf education, biodynamic agriculture, and anthroposophical medicine. Steiner advocated a form of ethical individualism, to which he later brought a more explicitly spiritual approach. He based his epistemology on Johann Wolfgang Goethe's world view, in which "Thinking ... is no more and no less an organ of perception than the eye or ear. Just as the eye perceives colours and the ear sounds, so thinking perceives ideas." A consistent thread that runs from his earliest philosophical phase through his later spiritual orientation is the goal of demonstrating that there are no essential limits to human knowledge".*

"Oh human, know yourself

This is the word of the world

You hear it powerful in your soul

You feel it overwhelming in your spirit

Who resists such world of power?

Who talk so ardently from the heart?

Does it go through the wide radiation of space?

In the experience of your senses?

Does it ring through the waving weave of time?

In the stream of your existence?

Is it yourself, like in the experience of space

Like in the experience of time?

Does word create you, while you feel a stranger?

The emptiness of the drum's soul

Because you lose the power of thought?

In the stream, that eradicates time

*Rudolf Steiner*

# Part Seven

## *Winds in the mountain*

Slowly my consciousness ceases to work.

The ray of light, again gets stronger

The metallic smell of a different reality appears again

I try to see

Memories of the spiritual world vibrate softly in my

consciousness.

All I ever loved, touch me like a spring breeze

All that is said or read is crystal clear in my

consciousness

The night is falling, and the stars shine bright.

All paths are telling me where they lead to.

The dust disappears.

It feels like I become closer to another world; the world where I once came from.

To enter the network of the trees, to go into their slinging, black and weaving wave, is somehow like entering death.

After I have observed, experienced, entered and lived within this living network for some years, I start to realize that the whole experience is an illusion.

#

I am in a deserted mountain landscape. There is no life. The rocks are barren and hard. I am walking there without knowing where I shall go. I am pulled up, up towards higher summits. The air gets thinner and I become exhausted. However, I walk on and on.

I can see a cross in the distance. A black cross appears, standing alone in this deserted mountain landscape. Now I have a destination. It becomes easier to breathe, and I get closer and closer to the cross.

After a while I notice there is something in the crossing point. ...

As I get closer I see that this is a rosicrucifix. It has 7 or 12 roses, sometimes 24, shaping a wreath around the crossing point. I get closer and closer, and soon I can differentiate the single roses.

The roses are stylized and immovable; sitting there untouchable, fixed to a black crucifix in the endless mountain landscape. I look at them for many days, until I get exhausted.

In my exhaustion, I reach for the hand of my lover. I hold my lover's hand ... and something miraculous happens.

Everything becomes alive; the ground of the mountain begins to breathe and move, as if it is turning into a plant, a wooden and living cover of wood.

Then the crucifix itself begins to change, gets brighter, begins to become alive, and then an eye appears .... seeing me.

After a while the roses also become alive, they grow, move, create bowls ... dripping nectar.

And I see that the whole energetic network of nature originates from this crucifix.

The complete, intricate, karmic and all embracing cosmos has its origin here.

The circle is closed. I lay down my pen, and feel that life is slowly disappearing.

Made in United States
Orlando, FL
26 February 2023

30415669R00036